The Story of Everglades City

A History for Younger Readers

Marya Repko

ECITY•PUBLISHING

Everglades City, Florida

PREFACE

This book was written for the students at our local school. It is a condensed and simplified version of my publication "A Brief History of the Everglades City Area". I have left out some of the details but added many more pictures.

I hope you enjoy learning about our history!

Marya Repko
Everglades City
March, 2004

The Story of Everglades City:
A History for Younger Readers

© 2004 text by Marya Repko
All rights reserved.

ECITY•PUBLISHING
P O Box 5033
Everglades City, FL, 34139
telephone (239) 695-2905
email: mrepko@earthlink.net

cover map from an aerial photo taken in 1926
courtesy of the City of Everglades City

set in Bookman Old Style, 12/16pt
printed in the USA
First Edition, First Printing April 2004

ISBN 0-9716006-1-9

The Story of Everglades City

CONTENTS

EARLY DAYS, 1859-1881 5
THE STORTER FAMILY, 1881-1921 7
LIFE WITH THE STORTERS 9
SETTLERS IN THE AREA 11
BARRON COLLIER, 1921 15
BUILDING THE TOWN, 1923-1928 17
LIFE IN THE TOWN 19
TAMIAMI TRAIL, 1923-1928 23
THE TRAIL IS OPEN! 27
DEACONESS BEDELL 30
TOMATO FARMING 32
LOGGING 35
THE NATIONAL PARK 37
THE CHOKOLOSKEE CAUSEWAY 39
THE END OF COLLIER 40
THE NEW CITY 42
TOURISTS 44
IF YOU WANT TO LEARN MORE 47
TIME LINE OF EVENTS 48

The Story of Everglades City

Courtesy of Florida State Archives

Map of Southern Florida in 1885. This area was part of Monroe County and Key West was the County seat.

EARLY DAYS, 1859-1881

This area was all swamp when it joined the new State of Florida in 1859. The only people living in the Glades were Indians. They were hiding from the U.S. Army because they did not want to be sent to reservations in the West. There were Army forts along both coasts of Florida. For example, Fort Myers was built to protect white settlers from Billy Bowlegs.

The Civil War began in 1860. Escaped slaves came to hide in the swamp. They made friends with the Indians, who taught them how to live in the wilderness. The black men taught the Indians to speak English so they could talk to the white men.

The other people who hid in the Glades were men who ran away from the Armies. They did not want to fight in the Civil War. Key West was on the side of the Unionists. It was an important harbor and was the seat of Monroe County. Northerners could go there and feel safe. There were a lot of men running away. They were sent to farm on Cape Sable. Some of them went from Cape Sable into the Ten Thousand Islands.

Two men who came here were the Weeks brothers. Their family lived in Virginia on a good farm. When the Civil War began, John was in New York on business. He was drafted into the Northern Army. His brother Madison joined the Southern Army at home in Virginia. One day, after a battle, Madison saw that his brother John had been captured. They decided to run away together.

The Story of Everglades City

By 1868, John Weeks was in Everglades City. There was no city then. He was the first farmer here that we know about. He cleared land on the bank of the river and grew bananas and sugar cane. The river was called "Potato Creek" because potatoes were growing wild along the river. Maybe they were planted by Indians or by other white men who did not stay.

One day John Weeks had a visitor. William Smith Allen lived in Key West He also had a farm on Sanibel Island where he grew castor beans for caster oil. A big storm destroyed his farm on Sanibel and he was sailing back to Key West. He ran out of water and food so he came ashore at the mouth of Potato Creek. He got help from John Weeks and returned to Key West.

William Smith Allen liked the good farm land on Potato Creek. He came back 2 years later, in 1870. He planted vegetables all along the river bank across from John Weeks and built a house. It was flooded by a storm in 1873. After that, he put the house up on stilts 6 feet high. This building was in the same place that the Rod & Gun Lodge is today.

He also changed the name of the river from "Potato Creek" to the "Allen River", after himself. He used his sail boat to take the vegetables to Key West to sell in the market.

THE STORTER FAMILY, 1881-1921

The next white men to settle on the river were the Storter family. George had been farming in Alabama. After his wife and one of his sons died, he took his two other sons with him in an ox wagon on the long trip to Florida. They went to Fort Ogden, north of Fort Myers. He soon swapped the ox wagon for a sail boat and began to explore the coast.

In 1881 George Storter sailed up the Allen River. He helped William Smith Allen grow cucumbers and tomatoes and eggplants. The vegetables went by sail boat to Key West where they were put on large steam ships going to New York. The next year, George's two sons visited to help with the harvest.

After that, George farmed his own land further up the river. In 1887, the two young men came to live with their father. One son was named George, Junior, and the other was Bembery. By this time, William Smith Allen was ready to retire. He sold his house and land to George, Junior, and went back to Key West. Bembery built a house for his family further down the Allen River on what is today Riverside Drive.

The brothers grew sugar cane at Half-Way Creek. It is called that because it is half way from the Allen River in Everglades City to the Turner River opposite Chokoloskee. Today, some of that land on Half-Way Creek is Plantation Island.

They brought the cane from Half-Way Creek to the Allen River in barges. Then they chopped up the cane and cooked it down into syrup. George, the father, made large tin cans in a little workshop near the big house. The syrup was put into the cans and sent by boat to Key West. On the way home from Key West, the boat was filled with supplies that they bought with the money from the syrup.

The Storter Trading Post and Home on the River in 1917.
Photo Courtesy of Florida State Archives

George, Junior, built a trading post and general store near his house. Indians came to sell skins from animals they hunted and meat from deer they killed. They bought things that they could not make themselves: brightly colored sewing material and guns and bullets. The store also sold groceries like tea and coffee and flour to local settlers. When someone wanted a special item, George, Junior, looked in the Sears catalog to order it.

In 1893, the little town got a Post Office. Bembery suggested the name "Everglade". He carried the mail on his boat. He sailed to Key West, stopping in Chokoloskee on the way with their mail, too. He also carried freight and, sometimes, people. There were no roads so everyone had to travel by water.

LIFE WITH THE STORTERS

George and Bembery and their wives had big families. The children needed a school. At first, the teacher used a room at George's big house. A one-room school house was built near the mouth of the river, but it floated away in a hurricane. Another school was built to replace it. There was no high school. Students who wanted more education had to move to Fort Myers.

The Storter Farm behind the Trading Post in 1915.
Photo Courtesy of Florida State Archives

George's son Neil even went to college. He started at the new University of Florida in Gainsville in 1907. He was 16 years old. During his first few years he did not study very much. In his last year, he became a hero. He was captain of the football team. His nickname was "Bo Gator" because he was from Everglades. The team soon got the name, too. It is still known as the "Florida Gators".

There was also a church in Everglade. At first, they held services in George's big house. Then they

The Story of Everglades City

built a little church. Some of the time they did not have their own preacher. A minister traveled around to all the little towns in the area.

Life was difficult. The people were real pioneers. They lived on the edge of the wilderness. There was no electricity. They had to collect water in cisterns for drinking and washing. They made wood fires to cook their food and to heat water for laundry.

George Storter's Store and Trading Post in 1917.
Courtesy of Florida State Archives

Rob Storter, Bembery's son, remembers that they never wore shoes, except maybe for church. Rob and his brothers and sisters swam in the Allen River, but they had to watch out for alligators. He sometimes went with his father on the sail boat to Key West.

SETTLERS IN THE AREA

By the start of the new century, the year 1900, there were a lot of people living around Everglade and Chokoloskee. They farmed on Sandfly Island and on the banks of the rivers. There were settlers living on Half-Way Creek, on the Turner River, the Chatham River and the Lopez River. Some of the names of the people are familiar today: House, Daniels, Boggess, Brown, Smallwood, Hamilton, and Hancock.

G.C. McKinney lived in Chokoloskee with his family. He moved there in 1886 and opened a store. He got the first Post Office there in 1891. He blew a horn made from a conch shell to let people know when the mail boat arrived.

McKinney was called the "Daddy of Chokoloskee". He was a very smart man. He could fix a broken bone and pull teeth. There was no real doctor, so he did all the First Aid. McKinney knew that learning was important. He got the County to send wood to build a school house. They also sent teachers. Life on Chokoloskee was difficult and the teachers did not stay long.

McKinney wrote stories about the people on Chokoloskee. The stories were printed in a newspaper near Fort Myers. We know about life long ago because of the stories he wrote.

Another important settler was Ted Smallwood. He came to Chokoloskee in 1896. At first, he helped a man named D.D. House with his farm on the Turner

River. In 1897 he married Mamie House and they moved to Chokoloskee island. He cut buttonwood to make charcoal that he sold in Key West.

The old Smallwood Store on Chokoloskee is now a Museum.
Courtesy of Florida State Archives

Smallwood opened a trading post and store. The Indians came in canoes to sell skins and furs. In 1906, he became Postmaster. The Post Office moved to his store. He also built fish houses in the bay. He kept ice in the fish house and the fishermen would leave their catch. The big boats from Fort Myers and Key West would pick up the fish and leave new ice.

Some exciting things happened on Chokoloskee island. In 1910, a man named Edgar Watson was killed in front of the Smallwood store. He had a farm on the Chatham River but everyone thought he was a bad man. There was a fight and he was shot. There was also a big hurricane in 1910.

The Story of Everglades City

In the summers, whole families would camp on Little Pavilion Key. They dug clams and sold them to the clam factory on Marco Island. Other families would camp on Chokoloskee to be closer to the good fishing grounds. The children helped with all the work. When they found a baby raccoon in the woods, they made it a pet like a kitten.

Sport fishermen also discovered Everglade and the Ten-Thousand Islands. They visited the area and stayed in rooms at George's big house. One sportsman bought land across the river and built a house for himself. His name was George Bruner and he was from Indiana. Before he came to Everglade, he went hunting in Africa for elephants.

In 1920, there was still no road. Freight and passengers had to go by boat. A road was started in 1914 to connect Tampa to Miami. It was called the "Tamiami" Trail because Tampa was at one end and Miami was at the other end.

Work on the road soon stopped because of World War I. The road only went from Tampa to Naples. On the east coast, it went from Miami to the end of Dade County. There was not enough money to build the rest of the road through the swamp.

The Story of Everglades City

Courtesy of Florida State Archives

Map of Southern Florida in 1893. Lee County was formed in 1887. Fort Myers was the County seat.

BARRON COLLIER, 1921

One man who could finish the road was Barron Gift Collier. He was born in 1873 in Memphis, Tennessee. He made a lot of money selling advertising in streetcars. When he was 38 years old, he visited one of his business friends on vacation in Florida. He fell in love with the Gulf Coast and bought the resort island of Useppa.

His friend also owned a grapefruit farm in Deep Lake, about 15 miles north of Everglade. The farmer had built a rail track from Deep Lake to Everglade to carry fruit to the boats on the Allen River.

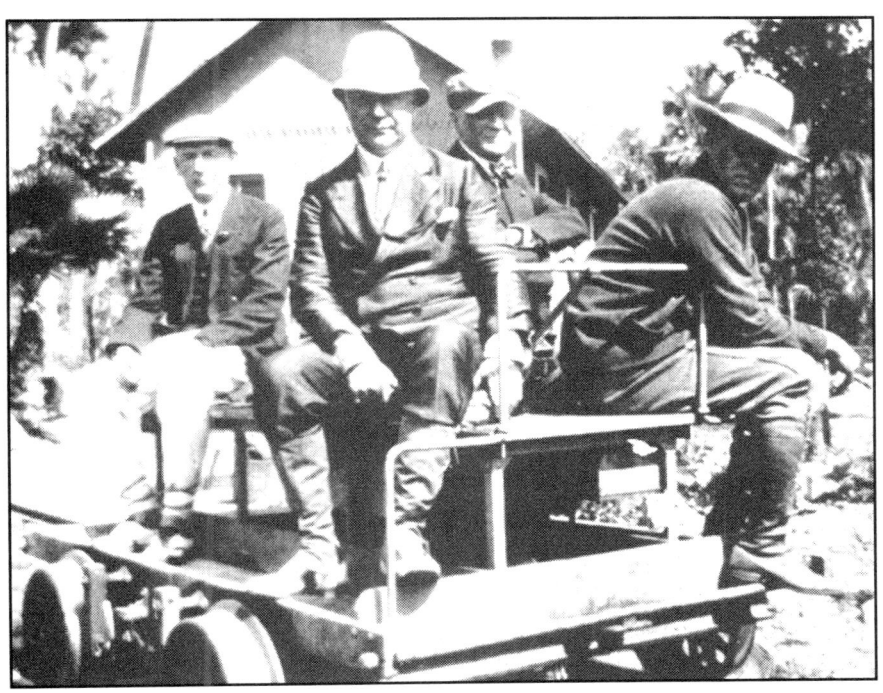

Barron Collier (center) on the Deep Lake rail car.
Photo Courtesy of Collier County Museums, Naples, FL

The Story of Everglades City

Barron Collier bought the grapefruit farm and a lot of land around it. Now he was interested in this part of Florida. He wanted the road to be finished so he could get his fruit to market quicker.

Barron Collier made a deal with the State government. If his land became a new county, he would find the money to build the road. The government agreed. In 1923 they made Collier County.

Barron Collier decided that the little town of Everglade would be the capital of his new county. He bought all the land and houses from the Storters. Then he changed the name of the town. He added an "s" to make it "Everglades"

The river was important. Ships could carry the supplies that he needed to build the road. He also changed the name of the river. Instead of the Allen River, he called it the "Barron River".

Barron Collier still had business in New York and other parts of Florida, so he hired an engineer to take care of things for him in Everglades. The new man was David Graham Copeland. He was born in 1885 in South Carolina. During World War I, he had been an engineer in the U.S. Navy. Barron Collier gave him two big jobs. D.G. Copeland had to build a bigger town and he had to build the road from Naples to Dade County. He also had to build a road to Immokalee and he had to make the Deep Lake rail track better.

BUILDING THE TOWN, 1923-1928

The land around the old Storter house was swampy. A big dredge took soil from the river and put it on the land. The dredge was called "Barcarmil". It was named after Barron Collier's three sons: Barron, Carnes, and Miles. The dredge also cut a straight, deep channel behind Pleasure Island for big ships. On the other side of the town, Lake Placid was dug out to get more soil.

D.G. Copeland planned the streets and buildings carefully. He fixed up the big Storter house and called the "Rod & Gun Club". Near it, he built offices for the men who were planning the road and a Post Office and telegraph office and a weather station.

Broadway looking from the River to the Depot in 1928.
Photo Courtesy of Collier County Museums, Naples, FL

Of course, D.G. Copeland did not do all the work himself. He hired engineers and carpenters and plumbers and electricians and builders. As the town grew, he added the Everglades Inn and the Bank and a Community Center and the laundry. He gave houses to all the families. They needed to buy food and clothes. He opened a branch of Collier's store, called "Manhattan Mercantile", downstairs at the Inn.

The new County needed buildings too. The sheriff had an apartment above the jail. The County Commissioners and the Court met at the Rod & Gun Club until the Court House on the circle was ready. We now use this building as our City Hall. It is one of our oldest buildings.

The Collier County Court House in 1928.
Photo Courtesy of Collier County Museums, Naples, FL

When the town was finished, about 5 years later, it was very pretty. There were flowers and trees along the roads. One man swept the streets every day. He also put up and took down the flag.

There was even a streetcar. It went on tracks from the north of the town to the Rod & Gun Club. The streetcar ran on electricity. It had big batteries. At night, it went to the electricity plant on Begonia Street where the batteries were charged up. Children rode the streetcar to school. It was free.

LIFE IN THE TOWN

A bigger school was built. The first students graduated from the new high school in 1928. A young teacher, Miss Ruth Neal, came to Everglades in 1926 to visit her father, who was an engineer working for D.G. Copeland. She stayed at the school until 1973. She taught the parents and grandparents of many children who live in Everglades City today.

The laundry building was ready in 1928. A big family did all the work. The men cut wood to make a fire to heat the water. The women did the washing and ironing. At night, they slept on the tables where the laundry was folded. They cleaned sheets for the Inn and the Rod & Gun Club. They also did the uniforms for the Collier workers. Barron Collier sent his own laundry on the mail boat when he was out of town.

The Juliet Carnes Collier Hospital was named after Barron Collier's wife. It had a doctor and several nurses who lived next door. If they could not help a patient, Collier paid to send the sick person to Miami. The hospital building and the homes are private houses today. They are near the Rod & Gun Lodge.

Everything in the town was run by Collier and D.G. Copeland. A whistle blew to wake people up. There were more whistles when it was time to go to work and at lunch time and when it time to stop work. Most people were paid in "scrip". This was Collier's own money. It could only be spent in his stores.

All the houses and buildings in the town were painted the same color. There were lots of trees and flowers along the streets. There was a goldfish pond on West Broadway and there was a monkey cage behind the Inn.

West Broadway. The old Post Office is on the left.
Photo Courtesy of Florida State Archives

People worked hard but there was also fun in the town. The Community Center held dances and showed movies. The drug store across the street in the Inn had a soda fountain where teenagers could meet.

On the Fourth of July, there were celebrations and games. At Christmas, D.G. Copeland put up lights and gave everyone a turkey.

Everglades Inn on Broadway and Allen Avenue.
Photo Courtesy of Florida State Archives

The Inn served very good food. It was cooked by "Snooky" Senghaas. He moved from Germany just to work for Barron Collier. People came to eat at the Inn from Copeland and Ochopee and Chokoloskee. The Inn also had offices upstairs and some apartments for workers who were waiting for their houses to be built.

The Rod & Gun Club was visited by important people. There were local guides on the river to take the guests fishing in the Ten-Thousand Islands.

The Story of Everglades City

Courtesy of Archives & Special Collections, Richter Library, Univ. Miami

Map of Southern Florida showing the route for the Trail.

TAMIAMI TRAIL, 1923-1928

D.G. Copeland was also working on the road. He put all the machine shops and heavy equipment in DuPont on the other side of the Barron River. Engineers there repaired the dredges and built trailers for the workers on the Trail. There was a sawmill to cut lumber for building the bridges. Most of the people who lived in DuPont were black. They had houses, a school, a church, and a recreation hall.

The land for the new road was all swamp and jungle. Some people from Naples wanted to drive to Miami. It took them 23 days. They had help from two Indians who knew the area. They had to cut down brush and push their cars through the mud. When the cars broke down, they had to fix them at their camp site. When they finally arrived, they were nicknamed the "Trailblazers".

Getting Ready for the Trail.
Photo Courtesy of Historical Museum of Southern Florida

The Story of Everglades City

D.G. Copeland had to raise up the land for the road. He got more dredges. They dug canals, throwing the soil to the side where the road would be. All the roads in this part of Florida have canals next to them. They are called "borrow canals" because soil has been borrowed from the canals to make the road higher.

Dredges digging up landfill for the roadbed of the Trail.
Photo Courtesy of Florida State Archives

Some of the dredges were called "walking dredges". They had legs and feet. The legs stood on either side of the canal while the soil was dug out. When one piece of canal was finished, the legs were moved forward to new ground. You can see one of these dredges at Collier Seminole State Park.

Other dredges were called "floating dredges". They floated in the water in the borrow canal. They could make the canal wider and deeper. The dredge

The Story of Everglades City

was so big that it had bedrooms and a kitchen for the men who worked on it.

The first road that was built went from Everglades to Carnestown. Now they could get supplies to the main route. A warehouse was built at Carnestown. It was called "Carnestown" after Barron Collier's wife. Her name was Juliet Carnes Collier.

Working on the surface of the roadbed for the Trail.
Photo Courtesy of Historical Museum of Southern Florida

As they moved towards Miami, the big dredges hit rock. There was solid limestone under the mud. D.G. Copeland got some dynamite to blow up the rock. It came by ship to Everglades and was taken to Carnestown. Then, it was pulled by oxen over the rough ground to the workers. He also got big drills to make holes in the rock for the dynamite.

The Story of Everglades City

CELEBRATIONS on APRIL 26, 1928

Parade of Cars on the new Tamiami Trail.
Photo Courtesy of Historical Museum of Southern Florida

Parade from the Bank.
Photo Courtesy of Florida State Archives

People greeting Barron Collier.
Photo Courtesy of Florida State Archives

THE TRAIL IS OPEN!

There was a big celebration on April 26th, 1928. The Trail was finally finished. On that day, 500 cars drove from Fort Myers to Everglades. Barron Collier was in the first car. They stopped in the town for speeches and some food. Then, they drove the rest of the way to Miami.

Everglades was full of people for the opening of the Trail. The first Collier County Fair was held. There was an exhibit of fancy motor cars in the big garage and plenty of food and games. The Collier County Fair is now held every winter in Naples at the Fair Grounds.

Collier County Exposition in Everglades in April 1928.
Photo Courtesy of Florida State Archives

A new bus service also made the trip. Collier had started the Tamiami Trail Tours Bus Line five years earlier. Before the road was finished, the bus only went as far as Marco Island. Passengers had to take a

The Story of Everglades City

boat from there to Everglades. The little bus company that Collier started became the famous Trailways bus line. Today it goes all over America.

There was also a new road and railway from Immokalee to Everglades. The old grapefruit track was made big enough for normal trains. They carried freight and people. The station in Everglades was the last stop on the line. After the train left the station, it backed into the neck of land that sticks out into Lake Placid. Then, it went forward and left the town. The station master lived upstairs above the station. Other rail road workers lived in cottages along the tracks. Today the old station is the Seafood Depot Restaurant. Some of the cottages have been moved into the town.

The Atlantic Coast Line Rail Road Depot in Everglades.
Photo Courtesy of Florida State Archives

The Trail was finished but it was not like a modern road. It was not paved and it was not very wide. There were a lot of wild animals along the Trail. Bears and deer and panthers stood on the road when a big rain flooded the land nearby.

The Story of Everglades City

Barron Collier made sure that travelers on the Trail could stop for food and gas. He built six stations along the road. Monroe Station is the only one left today. It is about 20 miles east of Carnestown.

Each station had a family to take care of travelers. The family lived at the station. The husband wore black pants and a red jacket and a big black hat. He looked like a Canadian Mountie, but he did not ride a horse. He used a motorcycle to patrol the road. He helped people who had trouble with their cars. The wife stayed at the station. She sold gas for 20 cents a gallon. She also had soda for 5 cents a bottle and made sandwiches for the travelers.

The Trailways Bus going near an Indian Village on the Trail.
Photo Courtesy of Florida State Archives

The Indians were not happy with the Trail. It cut across their hunting grounds. The borrow canal drained water from the swamp. They could not canoe from the coast into the forests. Some of the Indians sold souvenirs and snacks to travelers on the Trail and took tourists on boat tours.

PAGE 29

DEACONESS BEDELL

In 1933 a very brave woman came to help the Indians. She was a Deaconess in the Episcopalian church. Her name was Harriet Bedell. She was already 58 years old. Before she came here, she had helped Indians in Oklahoma and Eskimos in Alaska.

D.G. Copeland gave Deaconess Bedell a house on Camellia Street. She called it the "Glade Cross Mission". The house is still there, but more rooms have been added. It is across from our Post Office.

Deaconess Bedell in front of the Glade Cross Mission
Photo Courtesy of Florida State Archives

The Deaconess made friends with the Indians and visited their homes. She took their souvenirs in her car to the big cities and sold them to stores. All the money went to the Indians.

The Story of Everglades City

Deaconess Bedell and some Indians with her car.
Photo Courtesy of Florida State Archives

In 1960, the Glade Cross Mission was damaged by Hurricane Donna. Deaconess Bedell was safe but she decided to retire. She was 85 years old. She moved to an old peoples' home that was run by her church. She lived there for another 9 years. Before she died, she was busy helping the nurses with the other old people in the home.

Deaconess Bedell inside the Glade Cross Mission.
Photo Courtesy of Florida State Archives

The Story of Everglades City

TOMATO FARMING

After the Trail was built, people from Miami could visit the area. One man who came here was James Gaunt. He and his father bought land to grow tomatoes. The Indians told him that the word for "big farm" was "Ochoppee". That is what he called his new farm, but he spelled it "Ochopee".

He cleared the land and dug canals. The canals helped the water to drain during the rainy season so that the tomato plants would not drown. He also planted tomatoes along the side of the road because the ground was higher. He said he had the longest tomato rows in the country. They went for several miles down the Trail. He found that the soil on the north side of the Trail was better. You can still see the canals on the right along SR-29 after you cross US-41.

Gaunt built houses and a store and a packing shed. When the tomatoes were ready, they were picked and taken to the packing shed. Then, they were wrapped in tissue paper and put into boxes. The boxes of tomatoes were brought to the Rail Road Depot and went to the big cities.

In 1930, there were 250 people living in Ochopee. There was a restaurant and a boarding house and a garage. The new town had its own electricity plant. Ochopee got a Post Office in 1932. It was in the building with the store and farm office.

Most of the workers were black. They had houses in an area called "Boardwalk". It was behind

The Story of Everglades City

the store and packing shed. They had to walk on a boardwalk across the swamp to get to their houses. Gaunt built a school and a church for the black families. The white families lived on the other side of the Trail. They went to school and church in the town of Everglades.

Everyone worked hard. The men planted the tomatoes and weeded the plants and picked the fruit. The women and children carried water to the men. Mules brought fertilizer to spread on the plants. Sometimes the Indians came to help with the harvest.

Picking tomatoes at the Gaunt Farm in Ochopee.
Photo Courtesy of Florida State Archives

One night in 1953, a truck driver stayed at the boarding house. He was smoking a cigarette and he fell asleep. A big fire started. The boarding house and the store and other buildings all burnt down.

Gaunt cleaned out a little shed and used it as a Post Office. He was going to build a new store, but he decided to move all his workers to Immokalee. He stopped farming in Ochopee. The little shed is still the Post Office. It is the smallest one in the USA. Tourists stop and take their photos in front of it.

Old Picture of Ochopee Post Office and Trailways Bus Stop.
Photo Courtesy of Florida State Archives

Another tomato farm was started near Copeland. There were three brothers: J.B., Winfred and Wayne. Their last name was Janes. J.B. had worked with Gaunt and saw how well the tomatoes grew. They built their packing shed in Copeland near the rail road line.

The Janes men and their brother-in-law Alfred Webb built the store and the restaurant in Copeland. There was also a Post Office. Workers were paid in special coins with a "J" stamped in it. This was called "scrip" or "babbit". It could only be spent in the Janes store in Copeland.

LOGGING

The new road and railway from Everglades to Immokalee made it easier to get into the Big Cypress and Fakahatchee Strand. There were a lot of trees that could be cut down there for lumber. Collier had used some of the trees to build the bridges on his roads. Now other companies got interested in the forests.

Logging in the Big Cypress during the 1950's.
Photo Courtesy of Florida State Archives

The Story of Everglades City

C. J. Jones and his company cut pine trees in Fakahatchee. He built the little town of Jerome. His middle name was "Jerome". There was a sawmill and houses for the workers and a church. When the trees were all cut down, the sawmill was closed. The church was moved to Everglades. It is opposite the school.

Logging tracks leading to the edge of the forest.
Photo Courtesy of Florida State Archives

The Lee Tidewater Cypress Company cut cypress trees. The workers traveled by train to their work. They left early Monday morning to go to the edge of the forest and returned on Friday night. They kept building more track as they got further into the woods.

THE NATIONAL PARK

Some people were trying to save the plants and animals that lived in the swamp. They did not want more houses and factories to be built on Cape Sable or west of Miami. They said the Glades were special.

Finally, in 1947, the U. S. Government made the Everglades National Park. The National Parks Service bought some of the land. More land was given by the Collier company.

The President gets into his car after the opening of the Park.
Photo Courtesy of Florida State Archives

There was a big celebration when the Park opened. The President of the United States visited the town of Everglades. There was a parade. President Harry S Truman made a speech. Deaconess Bedell said a prayer. All the important visitors had lunch at the Rod & Gun Club.

People at the opening of Everglades National Park in 1947.
Photo Courtesy of Florida State Archives

Today Everglades City is the "Western Gateway" to the National Park. Visitors can rent a canoe and paddle all along the coast. They can stop and camp on the way. They can also take a short boat tour through the Ten-Thousand Islands and they can watch videos of wildlife in the Ranger Station.

If visitors go to the "Eastern Gateway" near Homestead, they can drive through the Park to Flamingo. There are boardwalks where they can see alligators and birds.

But, some local people are not happy about the National Park. The Park includes a lot of the water near the shore. They can not catch fish to make their living in the Park waters.

The Story of Everglades City

THE CHOKOLOSKEE CAUSEWAY

The people on Chokoloskee were unhappy. There was no road to Everglades. Teenagers had to take a boat to high school. In 1935, Ted Smallwood's wife Mamie got the County to start a road. It went where Plantation Parkway is today. But the work stopped. There was no money during World War II. A new road was started in 1954. It went along the coast. The road and the bridges were finished in 1956.

The dock and boat yard near the Smallwood Store in 1957.
Photo Courtesy of Florida State Archives

Now visitors could come to Chokoloskee by car. The local people built motels and trailer parks and docks for sport fishermen. There was a cafe near the Smallwood Store. In 1983, Outdoor Resorts bought three of the motels and they were made into one big trailer park with a motel and recreation hall.

Ted Smallwood was Postmaster until 1941. After that, his daughter Thelma ran the Post Office. She was Postmistress for 32 years. Another daughter called Nancy ran the store. The store closed in 1982. Today it is a Museum that is run by Nancy's daughter. It even has a cat called "Mister Watson".

THE END OF COLLIER

In the 1950's, Collier's company was loosing interest in Everglades. Barron Collier had died in 1939. Barron Collier, Junior, was the only son left. Samuel Carnes Collier died in a car accident in 1950 and Miles Collier died from a virus in 1955.

Barron, Junior, ran the Collier company with help from a man named Norman Herren. They tried to make it easy for farmers to buy land from the company. In Everglades, they helped people buy the houses that they lived in.

In 1953, the town became a City. The new Mayor and City Council had to take care of the roads and the water and sewer and electricity. In those days, the garbage collector was paid $1.00 an hour.

In 1959, all the people in Collier County had a vote about where the County offices should be. When Collier County was started in 1923, Naples was only a small fishing village. Now it had a lot of tourists and businesses. Everglades City lost the vote. The County got ready to move its offices to East Naples.

The next bad thing to happen in Everglades City was Hurricane Donna. On September 10th, 1960, the wind was over 100 mph and the water was more than 8 feet deep in the streets. The Barron River surged over its banks. People left their homes before the storm. Some stayed upstairs in the Court House. Other families got into their boats and went way up the small rivers, under the mangroves.

There was a big clean-up after Hurricane Donna. Some houses were blown over by the wind or washed away by the flood. All the money in the Bank got wet. When the water went down and the sun came out, the money was put on the front steps of the Bank to dry.

Cleaning up near the Inn after Hurricane Donna in 1960.
Photo Courtesy of Florida State Archives

The Collier company closed its department store at the Inn. Two men from Copeland decided to open a new store. Winfred Janes was already running Janes grocery and restaurant in Copeland. He and Carl Webb put their names together. They called the new store "WinCar". It sold hardware and dry goods. There was also a Sundries Store and a drugstore with a soda fountain. They all rented space in the Inn from the Collier company.

The Inn burnt down in 1987. WinCar built a new store but the other businesses closed.

THE NEW CITY

The County offices moved to Naples in 1962. The old Court House became City Hall. There was a lot of extra space. The City Council rented out some rooms to a woman who ran a gift shop. Another room was used for the library. Upstairs they held community meetings and dances for teenagers.

The Bank moved to Immokalee. The old Bank building was used as a boarding house for a while. In the late 1970's it became the office of a new newspaper, the "Everglades Echo". The people who started the paper also lived in the Bank. After they sold the newspaper and moved away, the Bank building was turned into a Bed & Breakfast. The guests could have breakfast in the old bank vault where the money used to be kept. Today the building is a vacation boarding house and health spa.

The City worked on the roads. They were all dirt. The Mayor found a company to put down paving. The families living on each street had to pay the company to pave the road in front of their houses. The roads were still dirt where there were no houses.

The City bought the land next to City Hall. The Lions club said they would help to make a park with a playground for the children in the city. They decided to call it McLeod Park. Daniel McLeod was the Mayor for 35 years. Before there was a City in 1953, he was the Mayor of the town. Now, he was retired and they wanted to thank him for all the work he had done for the local people.

The Story of Everglades City

McLeod Park opened in 1968. Five years later, in 1973, the people in Everglades City wanted to celebrate the 50th birthday of Collier County. They had an "old timers" reunion and a "little fish fry". After the fish fry, they bought equipment for McLeod Park with the money they had made. That celebration was the first Seafood Festival. It still takes place every year and the money goes to help people in Everglades City.

The old Laundry Building is now a Museum.
Courtesy of Friends of the Museum of the Everglades

The Women's Club had meetings in the old laundry building. The laundry business stopped during World War II because all the men went to fight. In the 1980's, the women wanted to save the laundry building. They had bake sales and raffles to raise money and they got money from the State to fix up the building. People gave old photographs and other old things to show our history. Now, Collier County takes care of the Museum but the women still greet visitors.

The Story of Everglades City

TOURISTS

Tourists have been coming to Everglades City for over 100 years. George Storter had fishermen stay in his big house. Barron Collier turned the house into the Rod & Gun Club. Most of the people came here to go fishing or to relax.

Tourist map from an old postcard.
Courtesy of Archives & Special Collections, Richter Library, Univ. Miami

The Story of Everglades City

In 1957, a Hollywood film company stayed here for three months. They made a movie called "Wind Across the Everglades". It was about the plume hunters and had a lot of big stars. Some local people had small parts in the film.

Other tourists stayed in the motel or in the trailer park on the Barron River. In an advertisement from 1953, the motel had rooms for $4.00 a night and the trailer park charged $1.00 a night.

The train stopped running to Everglades City in 1956. The railroad company said there was not enough business. Everyone used cars and trucks. The old station was turned into a restaurant. In 1968, it was bought by a man from Naples. He called it the "Captain's Table". He also built a hotel next door and docks on the Lake Placid for his visitors.

One of the men who worked in the hotel was called "Happy Harry". He loved to fly his little airplanes and would take people for rides. The airport was opened during World War II. It was sometimes used by the Collier brothers to come to work at their office in Everglades. Now visitors fly their planes here for lunch or to buy stone crab claws from the fish houses.

The Chamber of Commerce opened the Welcome Center in Carnestown in 1965. They rented the land from the Collier company and built the wooden store with the pointed roof. Tourists stop there to get brochures and to buy souvenirs and to get advice about what they can see in our area.

The Story of Everglades City

Today people still come to go fishing. They can rent a boat or go with a guide. Some visitors bring their own boats on trailers. If they catch any fish, the restaurants will cook it for them.

Fishing boat tied up at Chokoloskee in 1957.
Photo Courtesy of Florida State Archives

Visitors who are interested in wildlife can go to the National Park and to the boardwalk in Fakahatchee Strand and to the Big Cypress Preserve. If they are interested in history, they can go to the Museum of the Everglades and to the Smallwood Store in Chokoloskee.

Some visitors stay all winter. They are called "snow birds" because they want to get away from the snow. In the summer, they go back up North. When they are here, they go fishing and do things in the city with the local people. They like it here because the fishing is good and the town is friendly.

IF YOU WANT TO LEARN MORE

BOOKS TO READ

Crackers in the Glade by Robert Storter

Totch by Loren G (Totch) Brown

Florida's Last Frontier: The History of Collier County by Charlton W Tebeau

A Brief History of the Everglades City Area by Marya Repko

Historic Buildings around Everglades City by Friends of the Museum of the Everglades

WEBSITES TO VISIT

Historical Museum of Southern Florida:
www.historical-museum.com

Collier County Museums: www.colliermuseum.com

Florida State Archives: www.floridamemory.com

PLACES TO VISIT

Museum of the Everglades, Everglades City

Smallwood Store, Chokoloskee

Palm Cottage (Collier County Historical Society),
   12th Avenue South, Naples

Collier County Museum, Government Center, Naples

Collier Seminole State Park, US-41 near SR-92

The Story of Everglades City

TIME LINE OF EVENTS

STATE   LOCAL

1860-1865 Civil War
    1868 John Weeks settled here
    1870 William Smith Allen settled here
    1886 G.C. McKinney settled in Chokoloskee
1887 Lee County established
    1887 Storter Family settled here
    1896 Ted Smallwood settled in Chokoloskee
    1907 Neil Storter went to University
1914-1918 World War I
    1921 Barron Collier arrived here
1923 Collier County established
    1928 Tamiami Trail opened
1929-1933 Depression
    1930's tomato farming
    1933 Deaconess Bedell arrived here
    1939 Barron Collier died
1939-1945 World War II
    1940's Laundry closed
1945-1953 President Truman
    1947 National Park opened
    1940's and 1950's logging
1950-1953 Korean War
    1953 fire in Ochopee
    1953 Everglades became a City
1953-1961 President Eisenhower
    1956 Chokoloskee Causeway opened
    1957 *Wind Across the Everglades* filmed
    1960 Hurricane Donna
    1960 Deaconess Bedell retired
1961-1963 President Kennedy
    1962 County Seat moved to Naples
    1962 City roads are paved
1963-1973 Vietnam War
    1965 Carnestown Visitor Center opened
    1968 McLeod Park opened
    1973 First Seafood Festival held